FOOT PRINTS OF
GAUTAM BUDDHA

J.P. Sharma

Invincible Publication Pvt. Ltd.

Published By

Invincible Publication Pvt. Ltd.

For permissions, contact:
Invincible Publication Pvt. Ltd.
1103-A, 11th Floor, SAS Tower, Sector 38, Gurugram
Haryana- 122003
Phone: +91-124-4034247
www.invinciblepublishers.com

Sales Office: -4760-61/23, Basement, Pratap Street,
Ansari Road, Daryaganj, New Delhi - 110002
Email: invinciblepublishers@gmail.com

Title: Foot Prints of Gautam Buddha

Author: J.P. Sharma

Mob. 9415017239

Email: jaypeesharma@msn.com

ISBN: 978-93-86148-11-7

Printed in India
First Edition: 2016
Reprint: 2026

Buddhist Places in India

Contents

SACRED BUDDHIST PLACES

Buddhist Holy Places

Siddhartha, the royal prince meditated deeper and deeper, under a Bodhi tree (pipal tree) in Uruvella, on a full moon and realised that he knew the truth two thousand five hundred years ago. He had found the cause of sorrow and understood why the world is full of sufferings and unhappiness, how the mankind can overcome the miseries of life. He became enlightened–a Buddha.

Buddham sarnam gacchami, Dhamm sarnam gcchami, gacchami and sang-ham sarnam gacchami tre-ratna; three cardinal principles of Buddhism still continues in the several parts of the world.

Prince Siddhartha was born in Sakya clan of Kapilvastu while his mother Mahamaya Devi was going to home of her parents. This place has been identified as Lumbini in Tarai region of Nepal. Mahamaya Devi had a dream before the birth of prince Siddhartha that a white elephant was entering her womb. Royal soothsayers predicted that newly born child either would be the universal king or an enlightened one 'Chakravartin or Buddha.' Prince Siddhartha's mother died just 7 days after his birth; and he was brought up by his maternal aunt Prajapati Gautami.

There are differences among historians about the dates of birth and the death of Buddha, but most of the historians agree to it being in 563 or 566 B.C and death (attained nirvana) in 483 or 486 B.C. Therefore, he lived in 5th and 6th century B. C. which was the period of great intellectual movement in the world. Confucius and Lao-Tes in China and Zoroaster in Iran and were contemporary to Buddha and Maha-vira in India. During this period there were many developed cities in India and there existed Magadha Vaishali Kapilvastu Avanti Kalinga Videh Ang Kasi and Pava, well managed states..

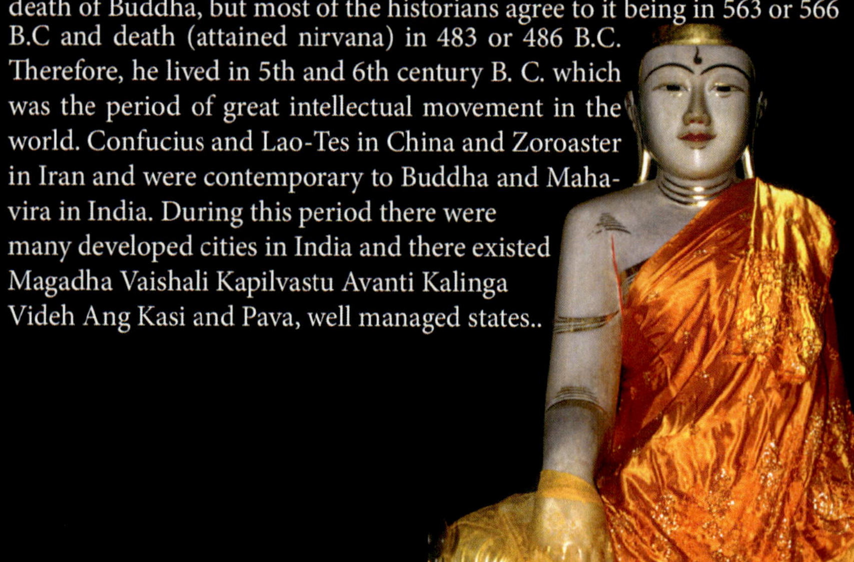

Utmost care was taken in the upbringing of Prince Siddhartha, all worldly pleasure was provided to the royal prince. Prince Siddhartha was married to a beautiful princess Yashodhara (Bhadra Kapalayani) of Koliya king. A son was born and named Rahul, as Siddharth considered his son an obstacle in his spiritual path, in spite of all materialistic pleasures, sighting of aged man, disease, and death realised him futility of the materialistic world. One night leaving his wife Yashodhara and Rahul asleep prince Siddhartha embarked upon in search of knowledge.

Siddhartha after leaving home practised austerities for about 6years. Alar kalam and Udrak Ramputra were unable to quench spiritual thirst of Siddharth. Siddharth practiced austerities, as a result of which his body became weak, and he realised that this is not the right path. One day while meditation he listened to a song being sung by the village women folk. The song meant that do not tighten the strings of veena (musical instrument) so much that they might break away and do not loosen the strings so much that it cannot produce music. Siddhartha realised the middle path (madhyam marg) is right path. He decided to have food, his five disciples thought Siddhartha had chosen a wrong path, therefore they left Siddhartha, he eat sweet rice (Kheer) given by Sujata a village women. On a full moon day in Vaishakha, a month according to Hindu calendar Siddhartha attained wisdom (Bodhi) and became Buddha. After attaining enlightenment at Bodhgaya lord Buddha decided to preach *dhamma* (new found sermon) to his five erstwhile companions who had left him. Therefore, Buddha came to Sarnath near Kasi present day Varanasi and preached Dhamma for the first time and this event in Buddhism is called Dharmachakra Pravartan (Turning the Wheel of Law).
Siddhartha was born in Sakya clan; hence his name is mentioned as Sakyamuni in Buddhist literature at many places.

Vedas held supreme power in the religious environment and Brahmins were sole custodians of religious activities. Caste system by this time had also become deep rooted in the society. Vedic rituals and animal sacrifice became an important part of the religion. In this religious atmosphere Gautam Buddha preached a new path of salvation which was very simple, he preached four Noble Truths (Arya SatyaChatushatya)this world is full of miseries (Dukkha), its cause is attachment (Samudaya), and suppression (Nirodha) of all these attachment Nirvana can be attained. Buddha preached eight fold noble path (Arya Astangika Marg) called middle path (Madhaamayam Marg) i.e. right view.

mindfulness and right meditation.

Buddha did not attach any importance to the problem of God and the soul because they were beyond the ken of human intellect. If a man desires to achieve the goal, he is cautioned to avoid involvement in complex and intricate matters concerning God and soul. If the moment he intricate himself, he is liable to forget his own self without solving his own problem. Buddha's approach to human liberation was unique in its own way and radically differed from all philosophical approaches or religious beliefs. Buddha travelled to the then existed kingdom of (Kosala and Magadha) situated in present day provinces of Uttar Pradesh and Bihar of Indian Union and propogated his teachings. After the demise of Buddha for more than two centuries Buddhism remained dormant. Thousands of killing in Kallinga war had a deep impression on the mind of Asoka, and saddened with tragic death, Askoka embraced Buddhism and abandoned war for expansion of his kingdom instead of this, adopted the policy of *Dhammavijaya* (Victory of religion) . As a result of royal patronage Buddhism not only flourished in India but it reached to far boundaries of Srilanka. Asoka visited holy Buddhist sites and erected stone pillars and built stupas at Lumbini, Sarnath Kaushambi, Bodhgaya and Vaishali many of them even exist today as a testimony of his faith.

Satvahanas in the south, though followers of Brahaminical in faith were tolerant of Buddhism and gave impetus to Buddhism. During the reign of Satvahanas Nagarajuna was contemporary of Yagyasri Gautmi. Nagarajurna was a great Buddhist philosopher and exponent of Buddhism in south India, the place has been identified as Nagarajurnakonda in district Guntur. Nagarajuna spent many years in Nalanda University also. Many scriptures written by Nagarajuna are available, translation of 20 scriptures in Chinese language have been preserved. Only two scriptures of Nagarajuna Madhayamik Karka and Vigrah Vyavaritini are available in Sanskrit.With the rise of Kushana dyanasty in India, Buddhism entered a new phase. Kanishka gave patronage to Buddhisim, during his time Buddhism reached to China and Central Asia. Gupta rulers were worshippers of Vishnu but during Gupta period art and archecture of Buddhist monuments attained new heights. Gupta rulers patronised Nalanda University which was a great centre of Buddhist teaching. Chinese traveller Fa-hein visited Nalanda University in 409 A.D. during Gupta period and Hiuen-tsang in 637 A.D. in the reign of Harshavardhan. Both the travellers have given a glorious account of Buddhism in India.
Traces of Buddhism are available till 1100 A.D. during the rule of Pala King of Eastern India. During the rule of Palla king Vikramsila University was a great centre of Buddhist learning.

Teachings of Buddha are preserved in Tripitakas in Pal namely: *Suttapitak, Vinayapitak and Abhidhammapitak.* Holy texts were kept in boxes *(Pitari or Pitak)* thats why they were termed Pitak. Pali tripitak are not of same time and same place. Pitakas was written at a different time and at different places. Pali was the language of Magadha Empire and Buddha preached his sermon in Pali, so they are regarded as Buddha Vachan authentic from the mouth of Buddha. Just 3 months after the nirvana of Buddha, a dispute arised in bhikshus regarding dhamma and vinay, first council (sangit) was organised in Rajgrah, second council was organised hundred years later in Vaishali wherein some dispute relating vinay were resolved. The third council was organised in Patliputra in the period of Asoka and in this council Pali Tripitak were finalised. Pali Tripitak found today is the same which was given final shape in the reign of Asoka. After third council Asoka sent his son Mahendra and his daughter Sanghmitra to Srilanka to propagate Buddhism. The fourth council was held in the reign of Kanishka in Kashmir. Since, the period of Asoka the two sects Hinyan and Mahayan arise in Buddhism. With the course of time Buddhism spread over beyond the shores of India in Nepal, Srilanka, China, Japan, Thailand, Korea, Burma, even nowadays where it is followed by millions of people. A large number of followers of Buddhism from these countries visit the Buddhist holy places in India every year.

Sacred Buddhist Places

Buddha became divine figure during his life time, after attaining enlightenment Buddha visited earstwhile princely states and performed some miracles, the places which had relation with the life of Buddha and the places where he performed miracles have become sacred spots to followers Buddhism. Four places which were directly related with events of life of Buddha are considered part of Dhamma Yatra. According to Mahaparinibban sutta Buddha told Anand each Buddhist is supposed to visit in his life time Lumbini in Nepal where he was born,Kapilvastu, where he spent early days of his life, Bodhgaya, where he attained enlightenment(Bodhi) and Kushinagara where he passed away, attained nirvana. Remaining places are Shravasti, Vaishali, Rajgriha, Sankisha, Kaushambi and Nalanda.

Lumbini

Main gate, to the Birth place of Buddha, Lumbini, Nepal

Birth place of Buddha is situated in district Rupandehi in Tarai region on the foothills Shivalik range of Nepal. It is about 20 kilometer from Bhairwana international Indo-Nepal border. Descriptions regarding the birth of Buddha are found in Buddhist literature. His mother had a dream one night that a white elephant having six tuskers entered in the womb of Mahamaya. Soothsayers predicted that child either would be a universal monarch or an enlightened one.

Mahamaya, the mother of Siddhartha, and the queen of Sakya ruler Shuddhodhan was the princess of Koliya clan. As per tradition of that time, queen Mahamaya was going to her father's home for the birth of the child. In way from Kapilvastu to Devdhaya queen halted in Lumbini garden, here she had labour pain, and caught hold to the branch of Sal tree and gave birth to the holy child named Siddhartha. Asoka visited Lumbini and erected a stone pillar to mark the birthplace of Buddha. Top of the pillar could not resist the ravages of time and weather, but shaft of the pillar still stands. The pillar is 24 feet and 3 inches long and radius of the pillar near the ground is 8 feet and 3 inches. In Pali it is engraved that Asoka visited this place in the 20th year of his coronation.

Adjacent to Asokan stone pillar there are ruins of monasteries which date back to 2nd century A.D. till 10th century A.D. A holy pond in which Mahamaya bathed the holy child after birth can still be seen there. In the later years a temple of Mahamya-devi was built near the Asokan pillar, this temple could also not resist the adversities of the time, and recently a new structure has come up encompassing the old structure. King Mahendra of Nepal erected a pillar of reinforced cement and concrete on historic site in vikram samvat 2020 on the occasion of Buddha purnima, When I first visited Lumbini in 1994 it was in miserable condition but during my second visit to Lumbini in 2014 I was unable to locate it in the crowd of recent structures. Nepal Government has enforced master plan of Lumbini which encompasses an area of 1.6X4.8 kilometre. Within a decade, a large number of monasteries of SriLanka, China and Thailand have also been built. Lumbini has become an international tourist hub along with the holy pilgrim centre.

Buddha Temple Lumbini, Nepal

Mayadevi Temple,(encompassing old structure) Lumbini, Nepal.

Asokan Pillar,Lumbini, Nepal

Ruins of Mayadevi Temple,Lumbini, Nepal

Ruins of Monasteries and Stupas,Lumbini, Nepal

Buddha Temple Lumbini, Nepal

Young Buddhists

Pond where Mayadevi is said to have bathed holy child Siddhartha.Image was captured in the year1993

Holy Pond Lumbini Nepal

Group of Buddhist people on Buddha Purnima,May 2014 at Lumbini, Nepal

Pillar erected in the honor of Buddha by king Mahendra of Nepal at Lumbini, Nepal

Shanti Stupa,Lumbini Nepal

Statues in Chinese Monastery Lumbini, Nepal

Kapilvastu

Ruins of Stupa, Kapilvastu, Piparhawa district Siddharthanagar, U.P

Capital city of Sakya, monarch Suddhodhan was Kapilvastu, there are differences in the opinion of historians and archaeologists regarding exact location of Kapilvastu. Some archaeologists have identified it as Piparhawa in present day Siddharthnagar district of Uttar Pradesh and some consider Tilwarakot in Nepal. Ruins of a stupa and some monasteries in Piparhawa district Siddharthanagar have been excavated by Archaeological Survey of India; artefacts found here strengthen the claim of Piparhawa as ancient Kapilvastu. Piparwaha is about 14 km from Lumbini, the site of Asokan pillar. Piparhawa is in present day district of Siddharthanagar in Utter Pradesh . This ancient site is easily assessable by rail, road from major cities of India.Nearest airport are at Gorakhpur and Lucknow.

Remains of Stupa Kapilvastu, Piparhawaha

Stupa Piparhawaha Kapilvastu

Sri Lankan Buddhist People at Kapilvastu, Piparhawaha

Ruins of Monastery,Kapilvastu Piparhawaha, Siddharthanagar

Ruins of Monastery,Kapilvastu Piparhawaha, Siddharthanagar,U.P

Bodhgaya

Mahabodhi Temple

Situated in Gaya district of Bihar, state of India, Bodhgaya is one of the holiest places for the Buddhists. Siddhartha practiced austuerites and penance for about 6 years in Uruvella on the bank of river Niranjana, which is presently known as Phalgu. In Ashad (month according to Hindu calendar) on full moon under Pipal tree (In Buddhist text it is popularly known as bodhi tree) Siddhartha attained enlightenment (Bodhi) and became Buddha. Numerous holy structures have been built in Bodhgaya during the course of time. As evident from the relief on the railing of Bharhut Stupa. Asoka visited this place, built Vajrasan, railing around the Bodhi tree and pillar with elephant on the top.

Alexander Cunningham was also of the opinion that present Mahabodhi temple exists on the remnants of Asokan structure. Mahabodhi temple dates back to 2nd century B.C. is evident from remains found from the site. Promenade (Chankam) is also considered an early structure. After attaining enlightenment Buddha walked up and down on this platform, it represents the lotous flowers which blossomed on his footsteps.

Chinese traveller Fei-Huen who visited Bodhgaya in 409 A.D., has described in his writings three monasteries. Hiuen-Tsang visited this place about the lapse of 2 centuries in 637 A.D. has described construction of this temple to Asoka. Mahabodhi temple had early connections with Srilanka, a Buddhist from Sri Lanka made contributions in the construction of a boundary wall of Bodhi tree. During the reign of Palla Kings, they contributed in the repair of the temple. In thirteenth century Burmese people also participated in the repair of the temple.

Mahabodhi temple is about 170 feet in height and its base is 50 feet wide, which consists of a straight pyramidal tower. All the four sides of the temple have several tiers of niches and front face has lancet opening for light. Present day structure of Mahabodhi temple is result of numerous restoration work carried out from time to time. On a niche above the entrance of the sanctum statue of Buddha has been placed and below foot prints on the rock on the floor have been carved, while entering the sanctum people offer flowers and coins as a mark of respect. In the sanctum of the temple there is a statue of Buddha in Bhoomosparsh Mudra –Buddha touching the ground.

After attaining Bodhi, Buddha spent seven weeks at different places, first week he remain seated under the bodhi tree. This original tree has fallen down and Alexander Cunningham brought a sapling from Sri Lanka and the present tree is planted by Alexander Cunningham. For second week he gazed on the bodhi tree, this place is animesh lochan, a stupa exists in the temple complex. Third week spent by walking on chankkam-promenade, he spent fourth week in ratangriha, fifth week under ajpal nigrodh tree, sixth week near Muchlind lake and last seventh week under rajat tree.

Engraved Foot Prints of Buddha, Mahabodhi Temple
Bodhgaya, Bihar

Back view of Mahabodhi Temple, Bodhgaya, Bihar

Stupa in Mahabodhi Temple Complex, Bodhgaya, Bihar

Buddha (in bhumi sparsha mudra) touching the earth,Mahabodhi Temple Complex, Bodhgaya, Bihar

Buddha Statue on a niche above entrance of Mahabodhi Temple, Bodhgaya, Bihar

Statue of Rahul son of Buddha Bodhgaya, Bihar

Trunk of ficus religiosa (Bodhi Tree)

Sarnath

Moolgandh Kuti Sarnath, Varanasi, U.P. India

Buddha came to Kasi (Varanasi) which was an ancient seat of learning; Isshapattn is 8km from Varanasi. Buddha delivered his first sermon, to five companions who had deserted him at Bodhgaya, which is called Dharmachakra Pravartan: Initiation of Wheel of law. At present this place is called Sarnath, here Buddha laid down the foundation of Sangha. In ancient times this place was also known as Mrigdav (place of deer). Another Sanskrit name of deer is: sarang, on the name of the lord of deer, later on it became popular with the name of Sarnath. At present State Government has developed a zoo near Mahabodhi temple, wherein mostly deer's are kept.

Asoka visited Sarnath and erected a stone pillar on the top of which four lion's were seated back to back, shaft of the pillar has been kept in the campus and top of the pillar has been kept in the museum situated at Sarnath. National emblem of the Government of India has been derived from this Ashokan pillar. Several other monuments were raised by Asoka at Sarnath important of them were Dharamrajika Stupa and Dhamekha Stupa. Dharamarajika Stupa was dismantled by Jagat Singh, Dewan of Raja Chet Singh of Varanasi in the year 1794.

While, the Dhamekha Stupa stands in its original form till today.

Dhamekha Stupa is a cylindrical structure, its radius is 28.50 meter and its height is 42.06 meter, up to the height of 11.20 meter it is decorated with geometrical designs, leaves and flowers. Monasteries have also been found there and Moolgandh kuti is the place where Buddha used to meditate. Present day Moolgandh kuti was erected by Anagarika Dharampala of Srilanka ,the then Secretary of Mahabodhi Society of India with the help of Mrs Mary Elizabeth Foster of Honolulu in the year 1931.

Another important structure is Chaukhand Stupa at Sarnath. It lies about half km from the main shrines, this is the place where Buddha first met his five companions (panchvargiya bhikshu) to whom he first gave his sermon. It is believed that it was a depleted brick structure stupa of 2nd century B.C. Upper part of octagonal tower was built by Govardhan, son of Raja Todarmal in 1588, while he was the governor under Akbar, to commemorate the visit of Humayun. Chinese, Japanese, Tibetan and Thai temples have also been built, recently in Sarnath.

Japanese Temple,Sarnath, Varanasi U.P.India

Dhamekha Stupa Sarnath, Varanasi, U.P. India

Buddha in Dharam Chakrapravartan, Mudra, Sarnath Varanasi,U.P.India

Dhamekha Stupa, Sarnath Varanasi, U.P. India

Chaukhandi Stupa Sarnath, Varanasi, U.P. India

Inside view of Moolgandha Kuti, Sarnath Varanasi India

Dhamekha Stupa Sarnath, Varanasi,U.P.India

Statues showing Dharam Chakrapravartan of five disciple at Sarnath Varanasi, U.P.India

Dhamekha Stupa Sarnath, Varanasi,U.P.India

Dhammama Sharanam Gacchami

Sarnath Varanasi, U.P.India

Modern Sharavan Kumar

Thai People practicing Vipassana,on Buddha Purnima at Sarnath Varanasi, India

Carvings on Dhamekh Stupa

Details of carving on Dhamekh Stupa, Sarnath, Varanasi, India

Volunteers at Moolgandha Kuti,Sarnath, Varanasi,India

Buddha in Chinese Temple, Sarnath Varanasi, India

Buddha in Japanese Temple Sarnath, Varanasi, India

Buddha in Tibetan temple, Sarnath Varanasi, India

Painting in Tibetan Temple Sarnath, Varanasi, India

Top of Asokan pillar displayed in Sarnath museum

Chaukhandi Stupa, Sarnath, Varanasi, India.Picture was taken 1994

Shravasti

Stupa Shravasti, U.P.India

In rainy season when rivers were flooded and roads were submerged in water and there were no highways like present days, it was not possible to travel, Buddha used to stay at one place. Buddha spent twenty four rainy seasons in Shravasti. Present day Shravasti has been identified as Saheth and Maheth. Recently, a district in the name of Shravasti has been carved out by State Government but archaeological site is 60 km away from Shravasti district headquarter, it is only 15 km from Balrampur district headquarters.

In ancient time, Shravasti was the capital city of Kosal kingdom, here Buddha performed miracles, once, a notorious dacoit Angulimal who used to kill people and cut their finger to make garlands, was also converted into Buddhism. Many of his sermons came from Shravasti. Shravasti is famous for one more reason, a staunch follower of Buddha purchased the land of Jetawan by spreading gold coins on the land. Many images and Buddhist deities have been found in excavations. When Fa-hein visited Shravasti he could see only ruins. The remains of Stupa and monasteries of Gupta and Kushana period have been protected till date.

Buddhist remains Shravasti U.P. India

Buddhist remains Shravasti, U.P. India

Buddhist remains Shravasi, U.P. India

Buddhist remains Shravasti, U.P.India

Vaishali

Asokan Pillar and remains of Stupas, Vaishali, Bihar, India

During the life time of Buddha, Vaishali was the capital of Vajjis, at several places there is mention of Vaishali in Buddhist text. According to Mahabagga of Vinaypitak Vaishali was a flourishing city; it had several palaces and kutagars. After becoming enlightened Buddha spent five rainy seasons in Vaishali, he has visited Vaishali earlier also. While making his last journey from Rajgir to Kushinagar Buddha halted here for some days it was here that Buddha announced that this is his last journey to Vaishali.

Vaishali has been witness to some other important events of life of Buddha. It was here that women were included into the sangha. State dancer of Vaishali adopted Buddhism and gifted her mangrove (amarvan) to sangh. Here even monkeys offered honey to Buddha. Licchavis erected a Stupa over their share of relics of Buddha, subsequently it was enlarged in Kushana period. Second Buddhist council (Sangit) was held at Vaishali and sangh was divided in Thervad and Mahasanghic.

Recent excavations conducted by Archaeological Survey of India have revealed remains of Kutagarsala, a swastika shaped monastery, a tank, number of votive Stupa and miniature shrines in addition to main Stupa and Asokan pillar. Asokan pillar is 11meter high with monolithic polished sand stone column surmounted by seated lion capital. It does not bear any edict of Mauryan period but few letters of Gupta period are engraved on it. Adjoining brick lined tank is seven tired measuring 65x35 meter in dimension and has two bathing ghats. This tank has been identified as(Markat Kunda) believed to have been dug by monkeys for Buddha, beads of semi-precious stones, terracotta figurine, seals, bricks embedded with semi precious stones and a terracotta figurine of crowned monkey were found during excavations. When the author visited Vaishali in 2011 excavations at some spots were in progress. The nearest airport is in Patna, though it is assessable by both rail and road.

Previsously, Vaishali was part of district of Muzzafarpur nowadays Vaishali is new district of Bihar state and it is about 66 km from Patna.

Shanti Stupa, Vaishali, Bihar, India

Survey of Buddhist remains at Vaishali, Bihar, India

Back view of Shanti Stupa Vaishali, Bihar, India

Rajgir

Shanti Stupa Rajgir, Bihar, India

Rajgir, ancient name Rajgraha, was the capital city of Magadh kingdom and one of the important sixteen great cities (Mahajanapada) during the time of Buddha, ruled by Bimbsara. Buddha spent several years here after attaining enlightenment, Bimbsara gifted Venuvan to Buddha. A large number of people became follower of Buddhism Sariputta and Maudalyagyan became the disciples of Buddha. Buddha displayed some miracles here, jealous cousin of Buddha Devadutta let loose a mad elephant Nalagiri at him, without causing any harm Nalagiri elephant sat at the feet of Buddha. Devadutta rolled a rock on Buddha to kill him, but Buddha stopped the rock with the finger of his foot.

Ajatsatru son of Bimbsara in his early life was not a follower of Buddha, he dethroned his father and put him in jail and got killed. Later on, this incident had adverse effects on the mind of Ajatsatru and he embraced Buddhism for mental peace. This incident has been beautifully depicted on Bharhut stupa. After the nirvana of Buddha, Ajatsatru got built a stupa on the holy remains of Buddha. Two centuries later after the nirvana of Buddha, first Buddhist Council was held at Rajgraha in saptikarni cave. Asoka visited Rajgraha two centuries later and erected a stupa and a stone pillar. Chinese pilgrims Hiuen-tsang and Fa-hein also visited here. Gridhrakutta hillock was the favourite place of Buddha here, when he used to meditate. Other important places to mention are Jarasandh ki Baithak, the ruins of monastery celebrated physician Jeevk, Maniyar math and ruins of cell where Ajatsatru imprisoned his father Bimbsara are also here.

Gradhakuta Rajgir, (a place where Buddha use to meditate) Bihar, India

Shanti Stupa, Rajgir Bihar, India

Buddhist temple Rajgir, Bihar, India

Sankisha

Remains of Asokan Pillar, Sankisha, U.P. India

Sankisha is situated in district Farrukhabad, Uttar Pradesh; its old name in Pali was Sankashya. Chinese traveller Hiuen-tsang visited Sankisha in 637 A.D. and had sighted a Stupa, stone pillars, temples and ponds, Alexander Cunningham identified this place in 1862 and in between 1876-1878 excavated this site, he has also mentioned about a stone pillar in Sankisha. This stone pillar is still protected here; at the top on inverted lotus an elephant is surmounted. The tusk of the elephant has been broken. Earthen ware, earthen pots for storage and several artefacts have been found, as a result of excavations carried out from time to time. Remains of a large stupa are here, local people have placed an idol of goddess named Bisheri Devi.

According to Pali text Buddha ascended to heaven from here to deliver Abhidhamma to his mother and afterwards descended along with Brahama and Indra on earth on this spot. During the time of Buddha, Sankisha was on road map from Kannauj to Mathura. A Sri Lankan monastery has been built there recently. Uttar Pradesh Tourism Development Corporation has established a tourist hotel also. The nearest airport is Lucknow from here you can reach by road.

Kaushambi

Buddhist archaeological site Kaushambi, U.P.India

Ancient city of Kaushambi was capital of Vatsa kingdom and under the reign of Udyan, who was a follower of Buddhism. Buddha visited Kaushambi several times. Fa-hein visited Kaushambi in the 4th century A.D. which he has described in his writings 'Kaushambi as great centre of Buddhism'. Asoka has erected stone pillars one of the stone pillar is still standing tall on ancient site, top of which is broken. Another stone pillar has been shifted to the fort at Allahabad. Instructions for Buddhists have been engraved on it. Ancient site of Kaushambi is spread over in the periphery of more than 4 kilometer. Ruins of a wall on the bank of river Yamuna have also been excavated. A district by the name of Kaushambi has been created, but ancient site is more than 15 km, from the headquarter. Kausambi is about 50 Kilometer from Allahabad and easily accessible by road from here. The nearest airports are at Lucknow and Allahabad.

Buddhist archaeological site Kaushambi, U.P.India

Buddhist archaeological site Kaushambi, U.P.India

Asokan Pillar Kaushambi
U.P.India

Ruins of fort wall Kaushambi,
U.P.India

Nalanda

Ruins of Nalanda University Bihar, India

Nalanda was prime seat of learning in ancient India, besides that Buddha visited Nalanda several times. Sariputta one of the famous disciples of Buddha was born here. Famous Mahayana taught person Nagarjuna was the chief priest of Naland. It is believed Nalanda name was derived because of abundance of lotus flower (Naal or Kamal) in the surroundings, some other learned people consider due to its great learning centre (naa alam dadatit Nalanda), there is no end to knowledge. Chinese traveller Fie-heuin and Hiuen –tsang visited Nalanda. During the reign of Gupta rulers Nalanda reached to its glory, coins of period of Kumargupta have been found here. According to mention of Hiuen –tsang, Gupta rulers built five monasteries here. Rulers of Pala Dynasty also contributed a lot for Nalanda University. Ruins of Nalanda University are spread over in the periphery of 4 km. Several artefacts found here are preserved in local museum and in many other museums of the country. Hiuen –tsang studied Buddhism in Nalanda University.

Muslim invader Bakhityar Khilji attacked Nalanda University in 1235A.D.-1236 A.D; and annihilated it completely, holy books and manuscripts were burnt out. Thus, glory of Nalanda University crept into dark for many centuries. It was Alexander Cunningham who brought it into the lime light.

Images of Buddha on stone Pillar Nalanda , Bihar,India

Ruins of hostel of Nalanda University, Bihar, India

Kushinagar

Ramabhar Stupa Kushinagar, U.P. India

Siddhartha was born in Lumbini, passed his early days in Kapilvastu, attained enlightenment in Bodhgaya and passed away in 483 B.C.in Kushinagar,at the age of 80, in the kingdom of Mallas. This incident in Buddhist text is known as Mahaparinirvana. Gautam Buddha preached his sermon at various places in Uttar Pradesh and Bihar Sarnath, Rajgrah, Vaishali, Kaushambi, Nalagram, Veranj, Shravasti. Buddha spent his last rainy season in village Beluva near Vaishali.

There is mention in Buddhist text, while leaving Vaishali, Buddha declared that it would be his last visit to Vaishali. In way from Vaishali to Kushinara, Buddha halted at Pava in the mangrove of Chund. He took pork meat, which caused infection in his intestine and developed diarrhoea. Suffering from sickness and pain he crossed the river Kakutstha and reached sal forest of Kushinara in the Malla kingdom. Feeling wearied and realising his end is approaching, Buddha asked his favourite disciple Ananda to prepare his bed under two sal trees.

Mallas of Kushinara paid visit to Buddha in his honour, a hundred and twenty year old mendicant Subhadra also paid visit to Buddha to pacify his spiritual doubts. Subhadra was initiated in Buddhism and he became last person to be initiated by Buddha. Last words of Buddha were *'Decay is inherent in all components, work out your salvation with diligence'*, he then fell into eternal sleep, attaining Mahaparinirvana.

For the six days his body was kept at state, Mallas made preparation of befitting funeral, seventh day he was cremated at a place what is now called Ramabhar stupa. The news of Buddha's demise spread far and wide and followers of adjoining kingdom, Ajatshatru of Magadh, Sakyas of Kapilvastu, Lichchhavis of Vaishali, Koliyas of Ramagram, Bulis of Alkappa and Mallas of Pava claimed the share over the holy ashes of Buddha. His ashesh were divided into eight parts and each of them erected a stupa in their region.

To commemorate these incidents, Mahaparinirvana Vihar and Makutavandhan Vihara were built in Kushinagara, which is supported from the seals discovered from the site, which shows the coffin of Buddha under the sal trees and flaming funeral pyre. For centuries this site remained unnoticed. Asoka visited this place and said to have erected a stupa at the site, archaeological excavations have supported this view. Emperor of Kushan dynasty also erected stupa and monasteries here. During the reign of Kumaragupta, shrines were erected. Archaeological Survey of India found a silver coin and copper plate which testified Nirvana Chatya and Nirvana shrine of Gupta period. When Fa-hieun visited Kushinara in between A.D.399 and 414, he saw a number of stupas and monasteries. Two centuries later when Hiuen tsang visited Kushinara, he found this place in a deserted condition. For many centuries this place remained unnoticed, for the first time Buchnn an officer of East India Company visited this site and mentioned the ruins. In 1854 H.H.Wilson identified Kasia as Kushinagar and finally Alexander Cunningham brought in light Kushinagar. Main site of excavations was Matha Kuar: site of the dead prince, Buddha, Alexander Cunningham found 10 feet 6 inches high statue of Buddha under a pipal tree.

Mahaparinirvana Stupa has a cylindrical base, the shrine houses 20 feet long statue of Buddha in Mahaparinirvan mudra, head facing the north and mouth facing west .This statue was established by Haribala in the reign of Kumargupta and present temple was erected after dismantling old structure in 1956. Voitive stupa monasteries, several other buildings and images were found around the site.

Mukutbandhan Chatya is the place where Buddha was cremated; it is now called as Ramabhar stupa. Hiranand Shastri exacavated the stupa and found some bricks of Asokan period which indicate that this stupa was erected by Asoka. Presently monasteries and stupa of China, Myanmar (Burma) and Thailand have been erected in the vicinity of the old shrine. Kushinagar is about 60 Kilometre from Gorakhpur and is connected with metalled road.

Buddha in Mahaparinirvana Mudra, Kushinagar, U.P.India.
Photograph of Buddha Purnima Celeberation

Buddha in Mahaparinirvana Mudra Kushinagar, U.P.India. Photograph taken 1995

Nirvana Temple Kushinagar U.P. India

Buddha Temple Kushinagar, U.P.India

Inside view of South Asian Temple,Kushinagar U.P.India

Inside view of South Asian Temple, Kushinagar, U.P.India

Sanchi

Stupa Sanchi, Raisen, M.P.India

Sanchi situated in Raisen district of Madhya Pradesh is 46 km from Bhopal. It is renowned for master pieces of Budddhist architecture that are visible in the large number of stupas and apsidal temples situated there. Although Sanchi has no apparent connection with the life of Buddha himself, yet it is closely related with the great exponent of Buddhism, Asoka. Numerous monuments, stupas, temples and a pillar erected by Asoka are situated in the hillock. The largest stupa erected by Asoka is the oldest stone structure in India. It is 36.5meters in diameters and 16.4 meters high with a hemispherical dome. This great stupa is surrounded by a massive stone railing and access to this passage is through four gateways or torana, that are a fine example of early classical art. The scenes carved into the pillars and the triple architraves are mainly tales from the Jatakas –the episodes of the Buddha's various lives.

Sanchi itself is little more than a tiny village at the foot of the hill. While climbing this hill one first comes across a hemispherical but smaller stupa with no gateway. It is significant because it contains relics of several Buddhist teachers buried inside that proves that has been a great centre of learning from 3rd century B.C. to 12th century A.D. There is another stupa that is significant because it contains holy relics of Shariputta and Maudglaya, both famous disciples of Buddha. The Asokan pillar is smaller than found at Sarnath but has proportionate and exquisite structural balance. Free standing columns erected from 2nd century B.C. to 5th century A.D. are situated near largest stupa. Besides the architectural pattern of a large monastery that resembles the ruins situated in Shravasti in Uttar Pradesh, houses a large statue of Buddha, inside a tower temple. Another temple constructed in the Gupta period was popular because of its flat-roofed square chamber with a pillared portico in front of it; this style was later used at the temples of Khajuraho and Odisha.

Gateway to great Stupa Sanchi, M.P. India

Great Stupa Sanchi, M.P. India

Matriye Buddha, Nubra valley Laddakh

หลวงพ่อ ไกลกังวล
नमो बुद्धाय

Lumbini

Nubra valley, Ladakh

Gangtok

Ladakh

Sarnath

Kushinagar

Rajgir

Rajgir

Bodhagaya

Nalanda

Bodhagaya

Nalanda

Bodhagaya

Lumbini

Sarnath

People of Faith